Star Gazing

by

Lula Mae Cameron

Copyright 2009 by Lula Mae Cameron

ISBN: 978-0-578-01949-9

All rights reserved. No part of this book may be reproduced or transmitted in any form or by any means, electronic or mechanical, including photocopying, recording or by any information storage and retrieval system without permission in writing from the copyright owner.

All poems written by Lula Mae Cameron
Cover designed by Jeffrey V. Taylor, Jr.

Acknowledgements

To my family: Many thanks for your love and support.

Contents

I'm Black 1
God Made Me 2
Slave Ship 3
The Best Gift 5
Star So Bright 7
Traps 9
I'll Pay the Cost 11
The Rugged Cross 13
February 15
When Spring Comes 17
Tell Me Why 19
My Lord Is Host 21
Little Ways 23
I Found Love 24
A Friend 26
Step by Step 28
Substitute 30
Courage 32
Sunset 34
Gospel Plow 35
Paid In Full 37
Spring 39
I Am A Missionary 41
Let's Make a Difference 43
Kids 45
A Broken Heart 46
Try Me 47
How Can I Get To Heaven? 48
If God Should Come 49
I Gaze Up Into The Sky 50
An Unseen Man 51
Somewhere 52

I'm Black

I'm Black! I'm Black!
Oh yes, I'm Black
And my skin has set me back.
God is good and God is great
He is first to treat me just.

I'm Black! I'm Black!
Please don't load my back
You wore my back with a heavy pack
You gave no slack, just made me track
'Cause I was Black, you packed my back
With a heavy sack.

From the break of dawn
to the setting sun
There was a pack upon my back
When the nighttime came there was
Only cramps and pain, no time for fun,
I could only lay and lick my wounds.

I'm Black and I'm proud
And I stand out in a crowd
I'm Black! Yes, I'm Black!
And I say it loud for all around to hear,
I'm Black! I'm Black!

God Made Me

God made me
It's not a crime
But, my slave master had no respect
Had no care and had no love
Made me mourn like a dove
When I was late, I got the whip
When I was blue, I got the stick
If I ran, he caught me again
Chained my feet, and cuffed my hands
I had no where to run or hide
I had no mother
I had no father
Not even a place to welcome me home
My native home, I had no more
Not even a friend to call my own
Not even my name was mine no more
My master's hate was a burden I bore
My master's scorn was something I wore
A stranger's face was all I had
Cramped inside and out
What a pain it all became
My teardrops ran down in leaks
'Til they made terrible streaks
I mourn and mourn for my dear mom
My father's arm I miss, so strong
I prayed and prayed for peace to come
But no such luck
But no such luck
But sometime soon I'll reach the sky
And search the clouds for my lucky charm
Free at last; free at last
From a hellish nation
And cuffs and chains

Slave Ship

This ship is sailing
But I'm not free
I was caught and bound
In irons and chains
Like a murderous criminal
And I had to do years of time
God in heaven knows it's hard
But I'll be free; I'll be free

I was put on a ship
Packed like sardine fish in a can
No room to shift, no room to sleep
Not even a place for my weary head
My body was cramped
My bones did ache
God in Heaven knows it's hard
But I'll be free; I'll be free

Now we sail and sail
Dull of mind
Nothing to do but stare and stare
Filled with pain, 'til it cramps my brain
My body bleed, my body swells
No doctor, no nurse; just a word of curse
God in heaven knows it's hard
But I'll be free; I'll be free

Then, they fed me slop to fill my tummy'
They fed me hate to feed their energy
They fed me a whip to break my skin
So I wouldn't run, or tell
But where could I go? I had no place, or no one
I had no cash, they made sure of that
God in heaven knows it's hard
But I'll be free; I'll be free

Now, I work from sun-up to dusk
Not a word of thanks, just "you stink"
What you fail to see is that you put me here
With a lash of your tongue
And the sting of your whip, you tore my skin
I have no love, you made sure of that
God in heaven knows it's hard
But I'll be free; I'll be free

Now, I go to bed
And dream and dream; but all my dreams
Become a lash of the tongue, a lash of the whip
Work from dawn to dust
No thanks, no pay, not even a smile
A word of curse is all I get
God in heaven knows it's hard
But I'll be free; I'll be free

The Best Gift

The best gift
is a good mind
to honor God,
and think of others
most of the time.

The best gift
is a gentle touch
that does so much
for the human race,
a gentle squeeze
that will hush a fuss.

The best gift
that my God gave
was my own life.
He gave in pain
upon the Cross
when he died
that I might live.

The best gift
was my two eyes
so I could see
what is planted
in the pathway
that I must trod.

The best gift
was my two hands
to use for others
when they have trouble
too hard to shoulder.
Then, I must bear
their heavy load.

The best gift
was my two feet
so I could go
that extra mile
to pull a friend
out of the mire.

The best gift
was my little heart
filled with love
so I could love
each and every one
in spite of all
they have done.

The best gift
was my two ears
so I could hear
God when he calls me
from labor to my reward.

Star So Bright

O' star so bright
I wish upon you with all my might
That you can shine a light
High into the sky
To guide my way tonight
Shine for me, O' star so bright

O' star so bright
I watch for you every night
Sometimes I sit and stare
Sometimes I take a peep
And close my eyes and sigh
O star, shine for me tonight

O' star so bright
What future do you have for me?
I know that you are wise
With light-years of wisdom
Won't you share some with me
To make my future bright?

O' star so bright
Share with me your stardust
To help me on my way
I know that I'll be blessed
With a hand full of stardust tonight
Be my star, O' star so bright

O' my star so bright
I think I'll sleep tonight
The sky is full of clouds
And I cannot see your light
But, I'll keep you in my dreams
And search for your light

And when I wake from sleep
Into the sunlight bright
I'll know with all my might
That you will shine again tonight
You will light up the sky
With all your beautiful light
O' My star so bright

Traps

All you trap setters
That set traps for others
Set one for yourself
For as sure as you see others deeds
God sees you

Your mischief could start as fun
But, before you are through
Someone may be hurt
And before too very long
You could be hurt too

All you trap setters
Don't point that gun at me
'Cause I'm standing nearby
Point it at yourself
Trouble is headed that way

All you trap setters
You set a trap for me
And set a trap for others
You can always see me
But can't see yourself

It may all be mischief
You are planning to play
It may be the cheapest trick
You ever planned yet
But soon it could cost you some bucks

All you trap setters
You may have planned it for a mere smile
Or a great big laughing joke
But don't you know that others
May not see it your way

All you trap setters
Learn to play it fair
Just think if it were you
Would you think that mischief was fun?
Or would you run and hide in fear

Stop these childish pranks
And act like grown-ups should
'Cause no sensible grown-up
Would play tricks like this
Unless you want to be caught, trap setters.

I'll Pay the Cost

If I treat you wrong
Just to do you harm
You can bet your arm
That before too long
I'll pay the cost

If you are lost and
Can't find your way
It is my duty
To show the right way
Or else I'll have
To pay the cost

If I misjudge you
For the wrong
No matter how long it takes
The price tag will hang around
Gathering dust and moss
'Til I pay the cost

If I lie to you for naught
Just to suit my every sort
Then my lie will cut me short
And make my life confused
Then I'll know it's time for me
To pay the cost

If I long to treat you right
And take time to give you respect
Then I'll realize the worthwhile fight
That God put forth with all his might
He paid the cost for you and me
With his life at Calvary

If I charge you with a crime
That you did not do
Then I'll pay every dime
'Til I repent
Then I'll know I paid in full
Just like Christ did upon the cross

If you need help in times of trial
And I'm not there
To pull you through
My work here is in vain
Then I'll pay the total price
I'll pay the cost I owe

The Rugged Cross

The road was crowded
On the way to Calvary
I'm sure that Christ
Felt so alone
But no one cared
A fearing crowd
With a heart of stone
The road to Calvary
Was long and hard
Every step he made
His heart felt faint
Silent teardrops
Not seen but felt
The road was rocky
And scarred the feet
Beady sweat drops
That dropped like rain
Drenched his body
Racked with pain
hot heat waves
That felt like a furnace
A heavy load upon his shoulders
Hard to bear, but bear he must
For little children in him put their trust
A hammer and nail
That broke the crust
That hurt and hurt
With force and hate
That pinned him fast
To a rugged cross
In mid air
With a sharp pierce
They speared his side
How could he endure
So much abuse?
But for me and you
He paid the price

By nailed hands
He bled and died
A brutal death
So we could live
He stood the test
Upon the cross
He rolled his eyes
Up toward the sky
And prayed a prayer
'Father not my will
But Thine will be done'
That's all it took
Jesus paid it all

February

February is notorious
It blows a beat and sings a song
Not a nursery rhyme I'm afraid
So baby can go 'night night' to bed
It's something like a monster's blow
That scares the wits out of you

February is dreadful
I hate to see the clouds roll up
Bust wide open
And make a flood
This puts me in a dreary mood
To match the mournful days

February is wet and soggy
Like a mud pie, it makes you dirty
Everywhere I step is mud
To stain my shoes that I wear to school
If February keeps this up
I can't be sure where I'll end up

The sun scarcely pierces the clouds
The clouds frown up
And soak the ground
There is water all around
And I'm afraid I'll fall and be buried alive
In a watery grave this side of the ground

I hope that March
Will bring a smile
The sun will shine and shine and shine
And dry the ground
Before I drown

They say that March and February
Occasionally exchange their days
I hope that March gives February
All its dreariness and its weary face
All its teary and drippy days
And say bye-bye to its dreary sky

When Spring Comes

I'll be so glad
When spring comes
Bringing smiles
And humming songs

I'll be so glad
To see the birds
Begging crumbs
Upon the lawn

The tweety birds
Standing tall
On two little legs
And making so much noise

The flowers blooming
In early spring
Pretty as pictures
In natures' colors

The bees and butterflies
Making their rounds
Filling their tummies
With the nectar of flowers

Green grass with beady drops
Showing its color
As the sun comes up
When spring comes

When spring comes
I'll be so glad
Bare feet and summer cuts
Will be the teenage fad

Spring is such
A joyous time
For all those that winter
Held in its rags spellbound

And now it time
To shed the rags
And enjoy the spring
And summer ahead

Tell Me Why

Why does the wind blow so loud?
Why does the bird sing so sweetly?
Why, oh why? Why, oh why? Please tell me why
Before I die.

Why do the clouds grow so dark?
Why does the rain fall so softly?
Why, oh why? Why, oh why? Please tell me why
Before I die.

Why does the moon grow so round?
Why do stars twinkle their eyes?
Why, oh why? Why, oh why? Please tell me why
Before I die.

Why do the sunbeams shine so bright?
Why does the sunset glow in the west?
Why, oh why? Why, oh why? Please tell me why
Before I die.

Why does the grass grow so green?
Why do the trees grow so tall?
Why, oh why? Why, oh why? Please tell me why
Before I die.

Why do the bees buzz and sing?
Why do the flowers bloom in spring?
Why, oh why? Why, oh why? Please tell me why
Before I die.

Why does mom laugh and cry?
Why does she bake a pie?
Why, oh why? Why, oh why? Please tell me why
Before I die.

Why does the bullfrog sit and mourn?
Why does the brook sing a song?
Why, oh why? Why, oh why? Please tell me why
Before I die.

Why does the ocean run so deep?
Why does the river run so long?
Why, oh why? Why, oh why? Please tell me why
Before I die.

Why does the night seem so dark?
Why does the light shine so bright?
Why, oh why? Why, oh why? Please tell me why
Before I die.

My Lord Is Host

Prayer is the key
To the Kingdom's shore
Where my Lord is host
As you enter the door

My Lord is host
And you are the guest
You are always welcome
And he serves the best

His dish is Love
He served it on the cross
For the whole wide world
To taste and see

My Lord is host
Blood for redemption
Water to cleanse
He gave his all
How sweet it is

My Lord is host
He gave in death
He gave his breath
That I might breathe
And have life Eternally

My Lord is host
He is now in heaven
Beckoning for you
And beckoning for me
To come and sit
At the welcome table

My Lord is host
He is serving Love
He is serving Peace and Joy
He is the host
And you are the guest
Taste and see
The sweetness of the Lord

Little Ways

If I can be a Teddy Bear
And bring some happiness
To some little girl
Or some little boy
Then I'll know I helped
In some little way

If I could be a spot of cloud
Nestled against the blue
I would not ask to be a rainbow
Just being a little spot of cloud
Would be enough for me

If I could be a rose
With a quiet beauty that charms
I would not ask to be a sunflower
That grows tall and handsome
I'd remain the beautiful rose
And quietly charm you

If I could be an apple
Big, pretty and red
And satisfy just one person
That took a bite of me
Then I would be content
To fill a small appetite

I Found Love

I found love
In a fashionable way
It wears and wears
But do not tear
It's built to last
Without the tears

I found love
In a memorable way
It went to school
And learned the rules
Even amid the blues
Love is cool

I found love
To be my O' so true love
It won't scrub off
And it won't rub off
No waste, no spills
It builds and builds

I found love
To be as peaceful as a dove
Pure and clean
No dirt, no grime
To make a slime
It lasts throughout time

I found love
And it's like a tree
First, the sprig
Then, the bud
Then, the leaf
And fruit to complete the tree

I found love
Without the toying
To ruin the mind
And break the heart
It stands in place
Without regrets

I found love
That can stand any test
I'm willing to bet
It is the best
No doubt in my mind
Every day life is divine
I found love

A Friend

You seem to know
When I'm sad
You lend an ear
And give a hand

You seem to know
When I'm upset
You hush my tears
And pat my head

You seem to know
When things are upside down
You stand your ground
And right the wrong

You seem to know
Just what I need
A friendly hand
A friendly smile
A friend indeed

You seem to know
When I'm in trouble
Your help is there
No ruffles, no feathers

You seem to know
When I am down
You pick me up
Placing me onto cloud nine

You seem to know
When I'm broke
When your payday comes
I get financial support

You seem to know
When I'm worried
Your words of wisdom
Is better then gold

Step by Step

You take life
Step by step
As you travel
Life's pathway
If you miss a step or two
You will have time
To regain your stride

When you take life
Step by step
As you climb
On your way up life's mountaintop
If one step falters
Then take a deep breath and try another
Then continue
On your way

When you take life
Step by step
If you miss your turn
Or your bend in the roadway
Stop still for a while
And steady yourself
Then steadily move forward
To gain another mile

When you take life
Step by step
Don't skip over or jump a step
Be careful where you walk
You could fall
Into a net

When you take life
Step by step
Don't get in a hurry
In the strides you make
Take your time
And be aware or you could end up
Being Satan's Imp

When you take life
Step by step
Don't you lean on so-called friends
Make your own decisions
And your own choices
Because friends could leave you
Alone to fend'

Take your life
Step by step
Don't make life too short
By following Satan's temptations
Or you could end up
In Satan's tent

Substitute

Love needs no substitute
It needs no mixture
To make a paste
Or make a batter
All it needs is
A place to bake
Love needs a kind heart

Love needs no tools to work
It needs no hammer
It needs no nail
It needs no saw
And needs no wrench
All it needs is a place to be
Love builds a room of its own

Love needs no substitute
It needs no prop
It needs no block
It needs no brace
To stay in place
All it needs is a place to stay
It will make a bed of ease

Love needs no substitute
It needs no soil
It needs no plow
It needs no water
To grow small seeds
All love needs is a heart
And you and me!

Love needs no substitute
It needs no lawyer
It needs no judge
It needs no jail to lock it in
All it needs is an invitation
To live with you and me

Love needs no substitute
Love is the big prize
Love cannot be replaced
Love mends,
Love defends
Love Holds

Courage

If I can have the courage
To shun Satan's ways
When temptation comes
I can look Satan in the face
And send him on his way

If I can muster the courage
To get through the day
Then when night comes
There will be no delay
In figuring out a way

If I obtain the courage
To pave the way
I'll be a role model
Then there will be no danger
In others falling along the way

If I can find the courage
To stop a lying tongue
Then maybe I could save
Someone from harm
And defeat a lying tongue

If I can envision the courage
To walk by faith
And live by grace
Then I can show others
How to see without sight

If I have the courage
To help the sinner man
To stop living in sinfulness
I'd show him the upper path
That leads to eternal life

If I have the courage
To shun the wrong for the right way
Then I would earn the privilege
To walk in the light
No matter how darken the night

If I have the courage
To give God my heart
Instead of letting Satan
Rule my little life
I can find the golden key
To eternal happiness

Sunset

There are only two of us
Gazing into the sunset today
You and me intertwined
We walk together
Hand in hand
Barefoot upon the sand
As we meet the outstretched tides
Our shadows clash and merge into one
Under the sunset sky
What a picture we two make
In the rose color of the sunset
Together we stand and watch
The setting sun
I begin to write a poem
Of the love we share
Bathing in the afterglow
As the sun hides its face
In the red western sky
Over the watery ebb and flow
Chilly winds began to blow
And waves dash to rocky graves
We slowly head for home
Looking back upon our footprints in the sand
Watching them wash silently
Into the white capped sea
Receding into eternity
How certain we two are
As sure as the evening setting sun
That our love will remain united
Until the close of that last day
When we shall gleefully part
And meet our Creator, God

Gospel Plow

Keep your hands
To the gospel plow
Be sure, be very sure
Every furrow you turn
Is turned in Jesus' name

Keep your hands
To the gospel plow
The soil you turn
In this earthly field
Could belong to you eternally

Keep your hands
To the gospel plow
Prayer is the key
To get into God's heavenly house
Love unlocks every door

Keep your hands
To the gospel plow
Lift voices loudly and sing
You are turning soil
With songs of praise

Keep your hands
To the gospel plow
When you give your tithes
You are turning soil
Give unselfishly
God will give back to you

Keep your hands
To the gospel plow
Don't tell lies
I must confess
You will give an account

Keep your hands
To the gospel plow
Don't let Satan
Guide your hand
Don't work in vain!

Paid In Full

This earthly house
Is like a company job
The main building
Is kingdom's shore
The main floor
Is in heaven's square
My boss man
Is Jesus Christ
When payday comes
I'm paid in full

The main officer
Is God Almighty
He'll sign you up
He is hiring now
His telephone number
Is a sincere prayer
When payday comes
I'm paid in full

There is no cut
From the wage you earn
Not even insurance
For the health problems you have
He takes care of those
With His healing balm
When payday comes
I'm paid in full

There is no cut
For income tax fees
At the end of every year
No counting your pennies
To make ends meet
'Til paid again
When payday comes
I'm paid in full

There is no cut
For household costs
For He owns your house
There is no charge
For doctors bills
'Cause God's got the medicine
In the hem of his garment
To cure your ills
When payday comes
I'm paid in full

Spring

Spring, I welcome you
With wide open arms
I'm sure that I can speak for others too
That you are our first weather choice
You were a long time coming
But, oh what a joy

You are in the nick of time
Before I climb' the walls
Old man winter
Began to tell on me
He kept me penned in
Between the four walls
I sit by my window
Watching old man winter
Spread his winter claws

Spring, I can tell you are on your way
'Cause I'm filled with joy
I know your little signs
Popping up here and there
Oh, I know there may be winds
That gives you chilly spells
But knowing you are there
Peeping through the clouds
Gives me the patience
To wait out the wind

Spring, I know that you are there
Just waiting for your entrance
To bring in the warmth
And move away the chills
And give life anew
To every living thing

I know you will be welcomed
By everyone including me
Because only you can erase
The harshness of winter's frown
You, Spring, have the power to rebuild
Whatever winter has torn down

I can almost see the sunshine
Rising with a smile
And going down all aglow
I can almost smell the earth
Thirsty for your showers
And I'm quite sure I can speak
For everyone abroad
Spring, you are truly welcome
And we greet you with a smile

I Am A Missionary

I am a missionary!
Do I have to tell?
Shouldn't it be visible
In everything I do?

I am a missionary!
Do I have to tell?
Shouldn't I show some signs
Wherever I go?

I am a missionary!
Do I have to tell?
Shouldn't it run very deep
Like water in a well?

I am a missionary!
Do I have to tell?
It should mirror gentle showers of rain
That falls in the spring

I am a missionary!
Should I have to tell?
I can lighten burdens
And carry God's Word, as well

I am a missionary!
Do I have to tell?
I may not have money
But shouldn't I give you my time

I am a missionary!
Should I have to tell?
Shouldn't I be like the rising sun
Spreading light all around?

I am a missionary!
Do I have to tell?
Shouldn't I be Christ-like
And give a helping hand?

Shouldn't I help the needy
Whose life has been defeated?
I am a missionary!
Do I have to tell?

Let's Make a Difference

We can make a difference
If we only try
We can pray a prayer
To help those in despair
We can sing a song
To help someone along
We can make a difference
If we only try

We can speak kind words
To help those who are discouraged
We can lend our minds
If we are wise
We can use our hearts
To help others, small and large
We can make a difference
If we only try

We can use our eyes
To help those who are blind
We can use our hands
To help across the land
We can use our feet
To trample down defeat
We can make a difference
If we only try

We can make a difference
Like night and day
It may be dark and dreary
But we can show the way
We can use our love
To unite the world
We can make a difference
If we only try

We can make a difference
Between right and wrong
We can make a difference
In our children's life
Give them love and care
To bring out the best
We can make a difference
If we only try

We can make a difference
In other people lives
By lighting a candle in the night
And sending out the light
Spread it all around
Without charge of a single dime
God is the answer
He will help you every time
We can make a difference
If we only try

Kids

Kids be good
Kids be kind
Please don't whine
You must behave
Don't be sassy
Or speak your mind
Be on time
If you don't listen
You could do jail time
Kids be good
And you'll be fine
Kids be good
Don't lag or drag
Sit up straight
And stand erect
Don't do bad deeds
Because others do wrong
If you do, it won't be too long
Before you find yourselves
Locked-up in some old place
Away from home

A Broken Heart

My heart is broken
Into bits and pieces
For the love we have misplaced
Come, let us gather together
To restring my instrument of life
Let's retune and make it strong
Like an eagle's wing feather
Fix my broken heart
For I know you meant to cause me no harm
My heart is broken
It has fallen from its place
Gently and reverently pick it up
Reset the bits and pieces
Steady its irregular beat
Blow off the dust
With the sweetness of your breath
Put my broken heart together again

Try Me

Try me Dear Lord
Just one more time
I confess
I'll do my best
To tend to your flock
Restore me Lord
I'll come back

Try me Lord again
I'll give my heart to you
And help those around me
Who are living in sin
I'll work to bring salvation
To some poor souls
I will defend

Try me Lord
And let my eyes
Become sight for the blind
I'll walk a straight line
I won't let them fall
Reach down Lord
And pick me up again

Try me Lord
Just one more time
I promise to keep my feet
On level ground
For I've drunk enough
From this bitter cup
Try me Lord, again

How Can I Get To Heaven?

How can I get to heaven?
You are standing in my way
Today and every day
Your work is of the devil
Your heart is full of evil
You are something like a weed
Choking out the good seeds
How can you lead me
When you don't know the way?

How can I get to heaven?
You are standing in my way
Each and everyday
Your work is of the devil
How can I get to heaven
Before the trumpet sounds?
Choose your own destination
But you are standing in my way
Especially today

If God Should Come

If God should come for you
Are you ready to go?
What a shame
To waste the Creator's time
How much valuable time did you waste today?
On whiskey, beer and wine
Stumbling and falling
Doing deeds not worth a dime
You were too busy
To show someone else the way

If god should come for you
Are you ready to go?
Shame! Telling lies and making a fuss
And never saying you're sorry
Never defending your kin
Just wallowing in filthy sin
And never making amends
If God should come now
Are you ready to go?

I Gaze Up Into The Sky

I gaze up into the sky
At all the pretty little stars
They seem to wink
And blink their tiny eyes at me
I never cease to wonder
Why God put them way up so high
Are they really exquisite jewels?
Are they there just to pretty up the sky?
What an awesome God
To make such a bundle of joy
I sit and gaze up into the sky
And I never seem to tire
I dearly admire the glittering stars
They're just small hunks of joy that
God fashioned and hung in the sky

An Unseen Man

As I walk alone
Among the many houses on the streets
Sometimes I sense fear
That causes me great alarm
I can feel pure hate
Lurking behind locked gates
Yet, somehow I get the courage
To go on my way
In spite of the lurking fear
I sense the presence of
An unseen man watching over me

Though I have done no harm or wrong
I must keep moving on
In spite of impending harm
Being forged by other minds and arms
I carry the gospel of peace
And even try to teach
Togetherness and harmony
So, as I walk alone
I am able to press away the fear
I am in the presence of
An unseen man watching over me

Somewhere

Somewhere, it will be fair
No rain, no sleet, no dripping snow
Only bright sunshine
No thief or robber can ever break-in
Safe and sound
In a secret place of mine
Somewhere I can sit and dine
Where no one else will disturb my peace
In the secret haven of my mind

Somewhere, it will be fair
No storm, no wind, can enter in
And damage or destroy this haven of mine
No sinful deeds will I have to plead
No troubles to make me worry or fear
Nothing to make me relinquish
Upon my head a starry crown

Somewhere, I will rest upon Jesus' breast
And never again worry about my life
No troubles shall blow over me
On ill winds from abroad
I'll have the very best
Success and peace
As I lay my head on Jesus' breast

I'll do my best to be a good guest
My only request shall be
Jesus, what does thou want of me?
Then I'll follow Jesus' commands forever more
Somewhere, somewhere
Around God's throne
I shall listen to His sweet voice saying
My child, welcome home

A NOTE ABOUT THE AUTHOR

Lula Mae Cameron was born in 1926 in Forkland, Alabama. She grew up in rural Alabama during segregation and the Jim Crow Era. Her parents were farmers and she was the youngest daughter of seven children. She attended Greene County Training School in Boligee, Alabama. In 1944, she married Amos Cameron. She is the mother of two daughters. Star Gazing is her first book of poems. Her writing has been shaped by her life experiences, dreams and vision for herself and others.

www.ingramcontent.com/pod-product-compliance
Lightning Source LLC
LaVergne TN
LVHW091320080426
835510LV00007B/577